HENRY MOORE
Mother and Child

FONTANA UNESCO ART BOOKS

Edited by Peter Bellew

Henry Moore

MOTHER AND CHILD

Herbert Read

COLLINS in association with UNESCO

© United Nations Educational, Scientific and Cultural Organization 1966
First Printing 1966
Printed in Italy by Amilcare Pizzi S.p.A. Milano

There are two distinct approaches to the work of an artist. One might be called historical, or at the personal level, biographical: it places the artist in his time and circumstances, and attempts to explain his achievement in terms of his social origins, his upbringing, and his relations with the artistic movements of his time. The other method concentrates on the art itself, as a series of formal inventions, and discusses the significance of that art from a wider point of view, a universal point of view. I have adopted the former method in relation to Henry Moore in my book *Henry Moore: Life and Work*; on the present occasion I propose to attempt the second and more difficult method, and assume that it is the method most appropriate for a publication with a world-wide readership in view.

The justification for this second method has been well expressed by C. G. Jung. In an essay first published in Berlin in 1930 and now included in volume 15 of the English edition of his *Collected Works*, Dr. Jung warns us against the common practice of reducing the work of art to personal factors, a practice which tends to deflect our attention from the work of art and focus it on the psychology of the artist. The work of art, he insists, exists in its own right and cannot be explained in terms of a personal complex. If it has any general significance, it meets the psychic needs of the society in which the artist lives and is therefore concerned with more than the artist's own destiny. " Being essentially the instrument of his work, he is subordinate to it, and we have no right to expect him to interpret it for us. He has done his utmost by giving it form, and must leave the interpretation to others and to the future."

This statement of Jung's clearly justifies the approach I am now going to make to Henry Moore's work, but the reader need not fear that I shall inflict on him one more essay in the psycho-analytical interpretation of art. In respect of Moore's work that has already been done, and done excellently, by the late Erich Neumann, a psychologist of genius. My aim is more modest. Accepting Jung's distinction between works of art that are based on materials drawn from the artist's conscious life, " his crucial experiences, powerful emotions, suffering, passion, the stuff of human fate in general," and works of art that come from the hinterland of his mind, " as if it had emerged from the abyss of pre-human ages, or from a super-human world of contrasting light and darkness," I shall assume that Moore's work is of this second, visionary kind and I shall try to give a reasonable explanation of its universal significance.

Jung's distinction between two types of artist is based on a wider theory of a collective psyche to which the visionary type, in moments of inspiration, has privileged access. All people have access to such a realm in their dreams, and a work of art is like a dream in that it presents an image from the artist's unconscious mind and allows us to draw our own conclusions as to its meaning. An artist is a man who can represent his subjective visions in tangible and perceptible form. To quote again from volume 15 of the *Collected Works*, " He has plunged into the healing and redeeming depths of the collective psyche where man is not lost in the isolation of consciousness and its errors and sufferings, but where all men are caught in a common rhythm which allows the individual to communicate his feelings and strivings to mankind as a whole."

One general feature of Henry Moore's work is immediately obvious on the most cursory survey—its confinement to relatively few themes. Indeed, if we give a very superficial characterization to these themes, it may well be that we shall conclude that the greater part of his work, perhaps more than three-quarters of it, is accounted for by no more than two themes—the Reclining Figure and the Mother and Child. From the moment that he was sure of himself and of his aims, Moore has concentrated on these two themes with an almost obsessional intensity. It is true that great artists in the past have often had the same obsessional limitations. Michelangelo's obsessions were of the same restricted kind, and there are artists of our own time who are even more obsessively restricted to one or two themes—Alberto Giacometti is an example who will immediately occur to the reader. But this is precisely the phenomenon to be explained, and explained in terms which do not obscure the problem.

I will first describe in more detail the nature of these obsessions in Henry Moore's case. I will then present any statements of his own which might throw light upon their significance, and finally I will attempt to give my own explanation.

Henry Moore was born in 1898, but owing to the interruption of the First World War his professional education was delayed for a few years, so that he did not complete its final stages at the Royal College of Art in London until 1924. He spent most of the year 1925 on a travelling scholarship which took him to Rome, Florence, Pisa, Siena, Assisi, Padua, Ravenna and Venice. He held his first exhibition in London in 1926, at the age of twenty-eight.

This first exhibition already included a figure of *Maternity* and a *Mother and Child*. There were in addition two *Reclining Figures*, one of painted plaster which was subsequently destroyed, the other a bronze. Most of the other themes were masks, heads, busts or standing figures—that is to say, all subjects directly associated with the human figure. Moore's work has remained predominantly humanistic in this sense, and we might say that whenever he has departed from the human figure, as in a few animal motifs, it has been to explore affinities or analogies with the human figure.

The human figure is, of course, the traditional motive of the art of sculpture, and only for short periods near the beginning of the history of sculpture and now in our own time has there been a variety of other motives. In the Neolithic Age the sculptor concentrated on ritual objects, axe-heads, maces, and other stylized weapons or tools used in religious ceremonies. In our own time a kind of sculpture we call " constructivist " has been evolved which equally owes its inspiration to tools (machines and architectural structures) and which is deliberately " non-figurative ", that is to say, non-humanistic.

The Greeks were the first sculptors to concentrate almost exclusively on the human figure. The reason for this is to be found in the whole Greek *ethos* or way of life, in which civic virtue is directly related to physical fitness, and beauty itself is identified with the ideal proportions of the human body (as the " ideal " itself is further identified with the harmony of the universe). The wise man, according to Plato, will always be found attuning the harmonies of his body for the sake of the concord of his soul (*Republic*, IX, 591). The body in Greek sculpture becomes a symbol, not only of physical perfection, but also of moral beauty—the fairest spectacle, as Plato puts it, being "; a coincidence of a beautiful disposition in the soul and corresponding and harmonious beauties of the same type in bodily form " (ibid., III, 402).

Throughout history man's ideals of beauty and of virtue have changed, but always a " coincidence " of these two ideals has been found in the human body. In Egyptian or Gothic or Baroque sculpture the human figure is modified to accommodate different dispositions in the soul: the form given to the body in sculpture becomes a mirror of the ideals of that particular civilization or religion. Instead of an ideal of " the beauty of reason " such as the Greeks held, other ages substitute the fear of the unknown, or a yearning for an absolute or transcendental existence, for some vital principle remote from human concerns. Our own age is anti-classical in this sense. We may appreciate the Greek ideals of harmony and serenity, but they do not " coincide " with our conception of reality. We therefore seek in art forms that have a convincing correspondence, and such forms are not likely to bear much resemblance to the forms of Greek sculpture. Yet still

Henry Moore in his workshop.

the human body remains the best " mirror " of the reality we wish to represent.

From the beginning Henry Moore was aware of this necessary correspondence between art and present reality (if the word " reality " seems to beg metaphysical questions, we may substitute " circumstances ") and in a well-known statement near the beginning of his career he declared: " Beauty, in the later Greek or Renaissance sense, is not the aim of my sculpture." He then offered his own explanation of this disavowal: " Between beauty of expression and power of expression there is a difference of function. The first aims at pleasing the senses, the second has a spiritual vitality which for me is more moving and goes deeper than the senses .... Because a work does not aim at reproducing natural appearances it is not, therefore, an escape from life—but may be a penetration into reality, not a sedative or drug, not just the exercise of good taste, the provision of pleasant shapes and colours in a pleasing combination, not a decoration of life, but an expression of the significance of life, a stimulation to greater effort of living."

In this highly concentrated philosophy of art we have the justification for the whole of Moore's subsequent stylistic development, based on what he had already established in the first decade of his work. Though as a statement it is clear and adequate enough, there are one or two phrases that may be more significant than the simple words would suggest, so I shall offer a brief commentary on them.

The whole philosophy of art implicit in the statement depends on a fundamental distinction between *beauty* and *vitality* as the " function " of art. This distinction, as formulated by Moore, no doubt derives from the ideas, if not the actual writings, of Wilhelm Worringer, which I, a friend of Moore, had been instrumental in propagating in England at this time (in 1924 I had edited the posthumous papers of a young English philosopher killed in the First World War, T. E. Hulme, in which Worringer's ideas were first introduced to the English-speaking public, and in 1927 I had succeeded in finding a publisher for a transla-

10

tion of Worringer's *Form in Gothic*). I am not suggesting that Moore was directly inspired by Worringer: Worringer in 1908 had intuitively discerned the nature of the revolution in art that was about to break out in Europe. He gave a theoretical formulation to ideas that were already in the air. I do not think Moore would have contrasted these particular words, beauty and vitality, if he had not previously been made familiar, however indirectly, with Worringer's thesis (which, briefly, is that the history of art shows that organic harmony is not sufficiently expressive for certain societies at certain periods of history: they seek a linear, inorganic basis for an art of heightened movement, heightened expression—what Worringer calls " the uncanny pathos which attaches to the animation of the inorganic "). But this, of course, is not an escape from " life "—life is not necessarily serene and joyful, but in many of its aspects vigorous, urgent, restless. The Greek ideal was to impose an abstract or sensuous harmony on this blind vitality; the contrasted ideal, which we might call Gothic, accepts this vitality as a virtue in itself, as a force that stimulates man to " greater effort ", as a means of expressing " the significance of life ", of penetrating to the nature of " reality ". No question of harmony, therefore, or of pleasure; just a question of psychological perception or penetration.

So much for the purpose of art. But sculpture is a craft and in order to fulfil the purpose of art it must conform to certain rules, or remain ineffective. What these rules are has never been stated more clearly than by Moore himself, in an article first published in 1937 and reprinted as " Notes on Sculpture " in *Sculpture and Drawings*.

Though strictly technical or practical, as they must be, it will be observed that these Notes begin with a clear distinction between what Moore calls the conscious and unconscious " parts " of the mind, and that the function he ascribes to the conscious part is to " resolve conflicts ", " organize memories " and " prevent the sculptor from trying to walk in two directions at the same time ". The rest of the article is for the most part a concentration on the problem of form or shape. He does not begin by

11

talking about something outside sculpture, such as physical fitness, or civic virtue, or even the beauty of reason; he talks about a perceptual problem, the problem of " comprehending form in its full spatial existence ". The sculptor must strive continually " to get the solid shape, as it were, inside his head ". He identifies himself with the centre of gravity of the solid shape and tries to realize, from the inside, the space that the shape is displacing. This process is sometimes called empathy, and it is the process that also takes place when a piece of sculpture is being contemplated. Shape, of course, is a very indefinite concept, and Moore next observes that some shapes are " universal " shapes to which everybody is subconsciously conditioned " and to which they can respond if their conscious control does not shut them off ". This is an important observation to which I shall return, but Moore admits that the forms he is most directly interested in are particular forms (such as the forms assumed by bones, shells, and pebbles, and above all the human figure). He does not give any further explanation for this preference—he assumes that it is a normal human reaction. But he does admit that the modern sculptor cannot confine himself to one form-unit, such as the human figure—he must relate and combine together into one organic whole several forms of varied sizes, sections and directions. His ideal is " a composition which has a full form existence, with masses of varied sizes and sections working together in spatial relationship". This somewhat Baroque conception of composition explains why, while recognizing Brancusi's historical importance in the development of contemporary sculpture, Moore finds his " one-cylindered " forms too simple, " almost too precious ".

Moore has some further technical observations on holes in sculpture, on the right physical size for a given idea, on the relation of drawing to sculpture, on abstraction and surrealism, but he concludes with a very significant statement which I shall not attempt to summarize: " It might seem from what I have said of shape and form that I regard them as ends in themselves. Far from it. I am very much aware that associational, psychological factors

Mother and Child. 1931. Height: 35.6 cm. Burgundy Stone. (Miss MacCaw Collection, London.)

play a large part in sculpture. The meaning and significance of form itself probably depends on the countless associations of man's history. For example, rounded forms convey an idea of fruitfulness, maturity, probably because the earth, women's breasts, and most fruits are rounded, and these shapes are important because they have this background in our habits of perception. I think the humanist organic element will always be for me of fundamental importance in sculpture, giving sculpture its vitality. Each particular carving I make takes on in my mind a human, or occasionally animal character and personality, and this personality controls its design and formal qualities, and makes me satisfied or dissatisfied with the work as it develops."

In other words, according to Moore his sculpture is " associational " in its purpose and content, by which he means that its form is determined by " habits of perception " evolved throughout human history. This is the kind of human art Jung described as " visionary ", and this visionary character of the art determines with directness and intensity the formal structure given to the material. Material, so often given as a determining factor in modern sculpture (" truth to material ") is thus interpreted as possessing an inherent form-potential, and a particular material is selected because it has organic vitality and can express more effectively than any other material the artist's vision. The material is not exploited for its own sake, but for the sake of the " sympathy " it displays with the visionary subject to be represented.

We are now in a position to consider why Moore selected two particular form-ideas as preferred subjects for his sculpture. It might, of course, be more exact to say that the form-ideas selected Moore; an obsession is not something we arbitrarily select—as in the case of a woman we fall in love with, there is presumably an unconscious propensity for this particular form.

The reason why, throughout the history of Western art, the human body in its natural state of nudity should have been selected as the central subject of art has often been discussed, but nowhere so perceptively as in Sir Kenneth

Clark's *The Nude* (subtitled " A Study in Ideal Form "). Sir Kenneth quotes Blake's *Descriptive Catalogue*: " Greek statues are all of them representations of spiritual existences, of gods immortal, to the mortal, perishing organ of sight; and yet they are embodied and organized in solid marble ", and this gives him the clue to the central truth, which is: " The bodies were there, the belief in the gods was there, the love of rational proportion was there. It was the unifying grasp of the Greek imagination that brought them together. And the nude gains its enduring value from the fact that it reconciles several contrary states. It takes the most sensual and immediately interesting object, the human body, and puts it out of reach of time and desire; it takes the most purely rational concept of which mankind is capable, mathematical order, and makes it a delight to the senses; and it takes the vague fears of the unknown and sweetens them by showing that the gods are like men and may be worshipped for their life-giving beauty rather than their death-dealing powers."

Spiritual existences can, of course, be symbolized by other means—by clothed bodies, as in Gothic sculpture, by distorted bodies, as in Byzantine art, or by geometricized figures, as in Celtic art. But nevertheless the human body is selected because it is " the most sensual and immediately interesting object " and it is such a subject for reasons which surely do not need to be emphasized. Not only is it always with us, the vessel containing our life, but it is the organ of all our perceptions and feelings. But the spiritual existences of which Blake writes are not necessarily beautiful: they are " death-dealing " as well as " life-giving " and though most men wish to live, and even to enjoy the illusion that life is everlasting, nevertheless, if art is to penetrate to the reality of life, as Moore thinks it should, then it should fearlessly represent those " spiritual existences " that threaten life. In a quasi-scientific language these spiritual existences would be called instincts, and if we accept Freud's hypothesis that there are two classes of instincts, we then find that he characterizes them as in effect life-giving and death-dealing. The life-instinct " comprises not merely the uninhibited sexual instinct

15

proper and the instinctual impulses of an aim-inhibited or sublimated nature derived from it, but also the self-preservative instinct, which must be assigned to the ego and which at the beginning of our analytical work we had good reason for contrasting with the sexual object-instincts. The second class of instincts was not so easy to point to; in the end we came to recognize sadism as its representative. On the basis of theoretical considerations, supported by biology, we put forward the hypothesis of a death-instinct, the task of which is to lead organic life back into the inanimate state; on the other hand, we suppose that Eros, by bringing about a more and more far-reaching combination of the particles into which living substance is dispersed, aims at complicating life and at the same time, of course, preserving it." Life itself is seen as " a conflict and compromise between these two trends " (*The Ego and the Id*).

Freud's formulation of this hypothesis has been much criticized, but it seems to me that it is fully supported by the history of art, which divides itself into two such general and contrasted styles, the one endeavouring to represent life, largely through its idealization of the human body, as a spiritual existence of sensuous joy, the other endeavouring to penetrate to the reality, which is not joy but conflict, not enjoyment but tragedy. But in both styles the function of art is redemptive or reconciliatory; in the one case offering the passive delight of ideal forms, in the other case offering a tragic paradox that can be clarified and sustained but never resolved in the tension of conflicting forms.

Moore is a tragic artist in this sense. He has never sought to idealize the human body, to make it the ideal representation of beauty, a stimulus to sensuous enjoyment. It is to be " an expression of the significance of life, a stimulation to greater effort of living ". But do such aims justify the kind and degree of distortion to which Moore subjects the human body? Are not these same aims fully expressed by a sculptor like Michelangelo without any comparable degree of distortion, and with complete respect for the human body as an ideal form?

this sense: the stress is on the human bond of affection between mother and child, and this is still true of the monumental group carved in 1943-44 specially for a Christian setting (the *Madonna and Child* in the church of Saint Matthew, Northampton). But already Moore is experiencing a conflict between the pathetic and the symbolic, between the particular and the universal. In a letter explaining his aims in this work he tells us that " there are two particular motives or subjects which I have constantly used in my sculpture in the last twenty years; they are the Reclining Figure idea and the Mother and Child idea. (Perhaps of the two the Mother and Child has been the more fundamental obsession.) I began thinking of the *Madonna and Child* for Saint Matthew's considering in what ways a Madonna and Child differs from a carving of just a Mother and Child—that is, by considering how in my opinion religious art differs from secular art." Moore then confesses that he does not find it easy to describe this difference in words; he can only suggest that a Madonna and Child should have qualities like austerity and nobility, and some touch of grandeur (" even hieratic aloofness ") that would be missing in an " everyday " Mother and Child.

In other words, pathos should be excluded. But the Northampton *Madonna and Child* is almost unique in Henry Moore's work, and though nobility and grandeur are words that can be used of most of his work, austerity and aloofness are missing from what is most characteristic.

It should perhaps be emphasized at this point that Moore himself does not belong to the introspective and self-analytical type of personality. He is not, except in a very general way, familiar with the theories and terminology of modern psychology or aesthetics. A critic is therefore justified in interpreting, or giving extension to, his rare and sometimes cryptic statements of his aims. For example, in the words just quoted he uses phrases such as " fundamental obsession " and " hieratic aloofness " that can be given a much wider significance while yet remaining still relevant to the work under consideration. It is at

Mother and Child. 1943. Height: 15.2 cm. Bronze. (Private collection.)

this point that we must resume contact with certain findings of depth psychology and see to what extent they illuminate Henry Moore's " fundamental obsessions ".

Personal obsessions of a neurotic kind are usually ascribed to some mental conflict whose real nature has been suppressed or disguised. An artist's obsession with a particular motif or form is not usually of this kind, and " obsession " may be a confusing word to use in such a connection. The motif the artist selects may have some personal significance for him, but such a motive only becomes generally significant, and on that account a work of art, if it captures what Jung called, in the passage already quoted, " a common rhythm ". It is this common rhythm that enables the artist, through his work, " to communicate his feelings and strivings to mankind as a whole ".

It is possible to interpret this common rhythm in purely materialistic terms—that is to say, as an aesthetic quality induced by metrical harmonies and proportions. Such works of art are necessarily of universal significance—the appeal of abstract art is of this kind, and an abstract element may be said to be present like a skeleton in every artistic " body ". But when the body is human the rhythm awakens feelings and associations that are no longer objectively harmonic (" attuning the harmonies of the body for the sake of the concord of his soul ", as Plato said); on the contrary, in visionary art they may be combined with feelings and associations that are essentially demonic. But there are good demons as well as bad demons—demons that promote life and demons that destroy life. There are demons that preside over the propagation of the species and others that ensure the fertility of animals and plants. There are demons that guarantee the immortality of the soul (guardian angels) and demons that would snatch the same soul to Hell (devils). But these demonic forces are not always personified; sometimes they exist merely as *tendencies* in the mind, and as such they motivate dreams and myths. To such innate tendencies Jung gave the name " archetype ", and in volume 15 of the *Collected Works* he defined the archetype as " an inherited *tendency* of the human mind to form representations of mythological motifs—representations that vary a great deal without losing their basic pattern.... This inherited tendency is instinctive, like the specific impulse of nest-building, migration, etc., in birds. One finds these *représentations collectives* everywhere, characterized by the same or similar motifs. They cannot be assigned to any particular time or region or race. They are without known origin, and they can reproduce themselves even where transmission through migration must be ruled out."

The Mother and Child is one such archetype, and the Reclining Figure is another. The Mother and Child motif appears first in prehistoric times; it persists all down the ages and the more it is stylistically transformed, the more it remains the same thing—an archetype of motherhood, of fertility, of the earthly propagation of the human species. Only a motif with this fundamental significance could have persisted for so long without becoming exhausted, without dying of inanition. It is sometimes stylized to such a degree that it is difficult to recognize its significance, and it is sometimes (often in recent times) so sentimentalized that it loses all significant power. But then comes a great artist, such as Giotto, or Michelangelo, or Henry Moore and restores the motif to its primordial significance.

The Reclining Figure motif is not so recognizable as an archetype, but it undoubtedly is one. Moore had discovered this motif early in his career—I have already mentioned the *Reclining Woman* of 1926. But about this time, on one of his visits to Paris, which took place almost annually from 1923 onwards, he saw a replica of the Mexican reclining figure known as Chac Moal, in Mayan religion the god of rain and organic fertility, on whose flattened torso (stomach) sacrifices were offered. Moore's great series of Reclining Figures followed from 1929 onwards to the present day, and in all its transformations the motif remains archetypal. But significantly Moore changes the sex of the figure, and introduces the suggestion of human fertility, which is then merged into an Earth symbol, the female body taking on the contours and rhythms of a

22

mountain range. Sometimes the body is excavated and within the hollow appears an internal form, a foetus. Finally the figure is divided, first into two and then into three separate forms, cliff-like and monumental, but related essentially to vital forces and to the altar upon which they are sacrificed to propitiate an Unknown God.

All Moore's other works are related more or less nearly to these two central archetypal motifs. Some are detailed explorations of bones or skulls; sometimes the mother figure is deprived of the child and at other times a second child is added, and even a father to form together a Family Group. Sometimes the reclining figure merges into mother to form an Upright Motif, which in its turn approximates to another archetypal motif, the Cross or Crucifixion. Moore's inventive spirit is like a fountain that is never still, that is always changing its form, and yet remains the same fountain, the Fountain of Life.

The Mother and Child motif, which has been chosen for illustration in this volume, is not so much propitiatory as celebrative. It takes the miracle of creation for granted, as not requiring a sacrifice to divine powers but rather a thanksgiving. The mother is idealized, becomes the Great Mother, the goddess of human fertility or fecundity; the Child is the symbol of genetic promise and continuity, of life renewed in each generation. In Christian iconography the Great Mother is the Mother of God and the Child is God incarnate, and both are " hieratically aloof ". But as an archetype the Mother and Child is not confined to the Christian religion: it is universal and is represented in the iconography of many religions. How universal it is may be learned from Erich Neumann's analysis of the archetype, *The Great Mother*, which is illustrated with reproductions from the Neolithic Age, from Ancient Egyptian, Mesopotamian, Cycladic, Minoan, Greek, Etruscan, Roman, African, Mexican, Peruvian and many other cultures.

Several aspects of the Mother and Child archetype may be distinguished: the Archetypal Feminine as deity; the Feminine force in Nature as opposed to the Masculine; the Feminine as the Great Mother indissolubly bound to the Child. Moore in his sculpture has represented all these aspects of the theme, but it is the mother-child relationship that obsesses him. It is for this reason that we have concentrated on this theme in the illustrations to this volume. It would be a mistake, however, to assume that Moore's approach to the subject is in any way systematic or ideological. Rather it is essentially human, and is not in need of an intellectual justification. It explores every direct aspect of the personal relationship—the instinctive dependence of the suckling child; the child clinging to the mother for protection; the child looking outward to assert its independence; the aggressive child, renouncing the breast that fed it; and finally the child reconciled in the unity of the family. All these are familiar attitudes, " the stuff of human fate ", and the artist's representation of them is based on observation, not on speculation. Nevertheless, and this is the measure of his stature as an artist, Moore always seeks the universal in the particular, and that, as Goethe once said, is the clue to the very nature of poetry, of all great art.

ILLUSTRATIONS

2

4

5

6

9

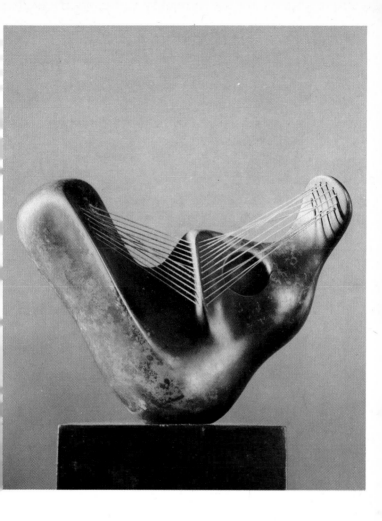

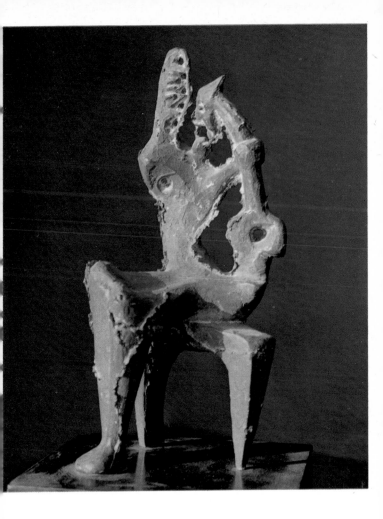

24